WASH, WASH, WASH YOUR HANDS!

By DAVID I. A. MASON

Illustrated by DAN WIDDOWSON

CANTATA
LEARNING

MANKATO, MINNESOTA

WWW.CANTATALEARNING.COM

CANTATA
LEARNING
MANKATO, MINNESOTA

Published by Cantata Learning
1710 Roe Crest Drive
North Mankato, MN 56003
www.cantatalearning.com

Library of Congress Control Number: 2014957036
978-1-63290-293-1 (hardcover/CD)
978-1-63290-445-4 (paperback/CD)
978-1-63290-487-4 (paperback)

Wash, Wash, Wash Your Hands! by David I. A. Mason
Illustrated by Dan Widdowson

Book design, Tim Palin Creative
Editorial direction, Flat Sole Studio
Executive musical production and direction, Elizabeth Draper
Music arranged and produced by Mark Oblinger

Printed in the United States of America.

VISIT

WWW.CANTATALEARNING.COM/ACCESS-OUR-MUSIC

TO SING ALONG TO THE SONG

Your hands pick up **germs** from the things you touch. Germs can make you sick. Washing your hands gets rid of many germs. Use soap and water, and then **lather** up for at least 20 seconds.

Now turn the page, and sing along.

4

ACHOO

If you use your hands to catch a sneeze

or dig into a pile of worms,

then make sure you wash them, please.

Your hands might be covered in germs!

So just wash, wash, wash your hands.

20 seconds is all it takes.

Just wash, wash, wash your hands.

What a difference to your **health** it makes!

Before you eat and after you blow your nose,
just try to remember this song!

Don't just wipe your hands on your clothes.
Wash your hands. It doesn't take long!

So just wash, wash, wash your hands.

20 seconds is all it takes.

Just wash, wash, wash your hands.

What a difference to your health it makes!

First you wet both hands plenty.

Then you lather up with soap.

Next you start to count to 20.

Lather, lather, go, go, gooooo!

1, 2, fast-forward now!

18, 19, 20!

After using the bathroom, stop and think.
Remember this simple trick.

20 seconds hand washing at the sink
can help keep you from getting sick.